THE INVISIBLE CROWN

A DEDICATION TO REV. DR. S. AUGUSTINE SATHIASEELAN

JEMIMA CALEB

ISBN 979-888546784-1

To the most honourable soul in Christ

Rev.Dr.S.Augustine Sathiaseelan., M.A., B.D., D.D., Ph.D., the greatest gift to us from Above, our well-wisher, guardian and strength, without whom we are not what we are today. I, along with my family, are eternally grateful to you, since you took in extra mouths to feed even when you didn't have to. You, with the most generous and selfless heart have put your dreams on the back burner to help us with ours, took pride in our achievements, held our hands through our disappointments, and stood by us during every struggle and all our successes silently. You were there for us when everyone, even our so-called relatives, turned their backs on us, and it is only your faith in us that still makes us want to rise like a phoenix to make you feel happy and proud. You taught us how to live in Christ, with discipline, tough care, manners, respect, and so much more that has helped us succeed in our lives.

We truly have no idea where we'd be if you hadn't given us a roof over our heads and become the fatherly figure whom we desperately needed to survive in this selfish world. You are the irreplaceable treasure, who is worthy of being treated like a king wearing a crown, whom my father, mother, sisters and I, as family earned all our lives, and no less. You are the only true source for all the good qualities and deeds that the world witnesses in us, and we are damn sure that you will be rewarded by the Almighty Lord in Heaven for all the good deeds you have done to us while you lived with us. We miss you to a great extent that no words can narrate, yet you are and will forever be living in our hearts, until we meet again on the next shore!

Thanking God for you,

Jemima Caleb.

Contents

Contents

Contents

Acknowledgements

First and foremost, I wish to offer my praises and gratitude to the Lord Almighty for the wisdom He bestowed upon me and for His never-ending Grace, mercy and the peace of mind, He provided for me to finish this book amidst the toughest times of my life.

I'm deeply indebted to Kashish Publications for rendering me an amazing platform to showcase the thoughts of myself and my co-authors to the readers. My sincere appreciation goes to Kashish Soni, who took this anthology under her wing, and responded to all my queries and led me on the right track.

It gives me much pleasure to acknowledge all my co-authors for the time taken to be a major part of this book and for giving me the authority to compile their works in this anthology. To all the members of this book, I thank you for your support, your passion, and your zeal.

Disclaimer

This anthology "The Invisible Crown" is an ideal mix of poems and tales of writers across the globe, reflecting their thoughts on optimism, hope, bliss and love, which gives the inner strength to the readers. All the writings published in this book are originally written by the respective mentioned co-authors. Any views or opinions are not intended to malign any gender, creed, religion, ethnic group or individual.

Neither the publisher nor the compiler would be responsible if in case the content is plagiarized, the respective writer will be solely responsible for the misbehaviour.

About Us

Kashish Publications is a growing platform for all the budding writers to fulfill their dream. It is founded by Kashish Soni, a budding writer who believe that writing is the magic to heal one's heart.

"YOU DREAM, WE ACCOMPLISHED!"

You can contact us for solo publishing or for compiling a one of our own.

Instagram id- @kashish_publications
Gmail- sonikashish004@gmail.com

About The Compiler

Jemima Caleb was born and brought up in Tamilnadu. From a very early age, she developed an immense love for the English language, which led her to traverse western countries just through her books. She is highly devoted to give her readers a fast-paced and sensational impact on life instances sure to melt their hearts. She obtained a Master's Degree in English Literature and today she is pursuing her dream of becoming a published author, and she remains interested in issues confronting young women who lack so many of the privileges that she now has by the Grace of God.

Having been brought up by a single mother since her late teens, she became increasingly aware of the plight of women that are commonly unnoticed by society. She has penned innumerable self-inspiring poems for readers of all ages, she loves to interact with people across the globe.

@jemima_caleb

About The Graphic Designer

Aanushnaa Bandyopadhyay is a 14 year old girl from Kolkata, who had her first view of the world on 2nd November. She wants to be a professional violinist and a great writer. She's a Manuscript Maker and Graphics Designer, which she chose as her recreational job. She loves to explore more, so she started making paid manuscripts after completing a few rough manuscripts of her anthologies.

She's currently the Brand Ambassador of a Reputed Publication and the Founder of Inking Hearts Writing Community. She has worked as the compiler of five books till date among which two came in the top 100 bestselling books on Amazon. She had also been a co-author of 130+ anthologies.

@bandyopadhyay.aanushnaa_2020

Compiler's Desk

1. Jemima Caleb

TO MY TREASURE, A POESY

My heart knew that God gifted me you as my Lear,
Your untiring and valuable lectures are always dear,
Even in my nightmares, your motivations I hear,
You understand even the language of my single tear.
The keys of my piano echo your fame,
The pages of my book mumble your name,
My thirst for knowledge from you it came,
And so, my gratitude will always be the same.
Who can say of your glorious majesty?
What can be compared with your honesty?
Can anyone elucidate your generosity?
Can anyone be an epitome of your nobility?
My lord, your magnificence will be praised with tendency,
Your name will forever be eternalized in my poesy,
My success in life will triumph your name with exultancy,
And my thankful heart will ever speak about you with courtesy.

Graphic Designer's Desk

2. AANUSHNAA BANDYOPADHYAY

BROKEN, YET A MOTHER

Totally Broken, she hailed to her house where her daughter was waiting with hope that her mother will return with her father after solving all their issues.

She just called her to ask when they'll return, but she had to lie to her that she'll return within few minutes.

How can even she tell her daughter that her father will never return to them, as he found a new wife for him? How can she tell her, that her father cheated them and transferred all the money to her new lover's name…!

Immersed in her thoughts, she didn't realised when she reached her house. She rung the bell, her daughter came running with the joy to see her father.

But all her happiness fade away, seeing her mother, rather only her mother on the door. She was very angry on her, passing the door keys, her daughter sat on the couch, with a grumpy face!

Now, it was her turn to make her daughter believe her excuses. But even after continuing their talk for more than one hour, she wasn't able to calm her daughter. Her angry daughter, went to her room, making a loud sound with her feets to get the attention.

After that day, it was nearly two weeks, everyday her daughter would ask for her father, and at the last, she would turn her down. Day by Day, their bond was breaking and also they stopped talking to each other nicely!

One day, her daughter was returning from her school, when she spotted her father with another woman. She got more angry, she went to her and started scolding him for not returning.

Her father didn't knew that she was unaware of the whole thing. He told her that he left her and her mother and that he also took all their money.

She was dumbstruck. All this time, she had been thinking that her mother was keeping her father away from her, because she didn't loved her, but the thing was its opposite!

All this time, her mother was preventing her from the harsh truth of their life. Returning her house, she ran to her mother and hugged her. She told her everything that happened today and also apologized, and they two lived together happily ever after.

Now don't ask me how they managed without money?! As even if you don't have anything, a support of your own can motivate you to regain all those things again!

Co-author's Desk

3. Jehosheba Caleb

Jehosheba Caleb is a lifelong learner and bibliophile, who was born and brought up in Tamil Nadu, India. As she grew older, she progressed in writing poems, and developed a firm faith in Christ and a keen interest in literature and poetry. She lost hope in humans but not in her God, Who watches over her every millisecond. Her writings on life, love, untold miseries, and the inner beauty of human beings inspired many hearts to remain strong and brave amidst the trials and tribulations of the world, and serve up a feast of insight for her readers and listeners. Her passion is to become a published author and at present, she's working on it tirelessly. She embraces reading books as her escape from the real world. She loves to interact with her readers across the world.

@caesar6736

LOVE OF MY FATHER

You raised me by your sacrifices,
But I can't even sacrifice my life
For you.
You consoled me when my
Eyes welled with tears,
But I left you when your eyes
Are filled with tears and fears.
You gave me a good education
In your hardest part of the days,

But I failed to give you the best
Hospitality.
You gave me a belief of how
Deep a man can love her daughter,
But I failed to show you how a
Daughter can watch over her
Father in his darkest days.
People said,"I definitely have
A better future".
I sighed, "Yes, better future
Without the one who raised
Me by his sacrifices and
Struggles".

4. PREETI KUMARI

Preeti is a student who is an introvert by nature. She is from Samstipur, Bihar, and she is the daughter of Surendra Kumar and Kumari Mala. She started writing during a pandemic that occurred in India. She loves to write about life and women's issues and equality.
@Preet_poem

STAY WITH ME

Stay a little longer with me ?be with me some more time .I know we will part away let me make some memories which never fade away. Wanna life again with you , be the part of my life ,lots of hustle in my mind I will express along with you wanna stay with like sun and moon . Am all yours do with me what you u want?

Ask why I am disappearing like a rain,

All your prayer got in vain ,

Come closer but little slower,

Stay a little longer with me,

For some more time,

It's my time to leave u alone,

Punish me , how u want

I know u can't live without me,

It's not my choice to leave u alone,

It's a god call from beautiful heaven,

We will meet their after some time,

May you live a happy life,

Don't think about I will find your memories and talk with you whole my life.

I will stay by your side

Please forget me like a dreadful night.

Live again and grab all your happiness.

You will be always the best part of my life.

5. S. BLESSY EVANGELINE

Blessy Evangeline was born and brought up in Tamil Nadu. She's fond of poetry and passionate about literature. She was inspired to become a writer after becoming frustrated at the endings to some of his favourite books, and she started writing at the age of fourteen. As she grew older, she progressed to writing more articles. She took a keen interest in search of humanity in human. Her writing is based on the theme of kindling the heart of readers to be strong in realistic life rather than on imaginary.

LIFE

Life is once

Doesn't awake twice.

The sun Dawn in the morning

And down in the evening.

Life may come and may go

Like a sea waves on the seashore.

According to catechism,

Life is Like a flower,smoke,green bushes.

And is full of sombre and excites

Life is to be happy.

Life may come and may go

Let's grasp our life to live with cheer.

6. Priya Das

Priya Das is passionate about writing and paintings. She is a trained artist, calligrapher and published writer. She loves to play with beautiful words and is fond of reading books. Her writings portray a contrast of nature and a glimpse of the reality of life. At present, she is pursuing BSc in Biotechnology.

@the_poet_gallery

ENDLESS LOVE

My eyes seek for your love in the smoggy past memories…In the soothing warm breeze…

I build a magical castle for you from the feelings of my deepest core.

Located in the edge of my heart beside the sea shore.

On flying clouds in the bright sky, You will always stay in my eyes.

You poured desires in my heart.

Don't break my feelings into parts.

The soft touch of your love made the flowers to bloom…

In the dazzling full-moon.

My wandering hopes gets lighten in the warmth of your feelings.

Through the isolated road of your memories.

My whole world is framed within you.

All along I believed destiny has brought your heart to me.

7. JYOTIKA SA

Words are the swords of your thoughts. Jyotika Sa is from Odisha and she's a Biotech student. Her dream is to be a scientist BT and she's having my passion towards exploring words .
@Sajyotika

BEING WITH YOU
Life gets better when,
I see you with me
I feel like an angel when you
Treat me as with care
I found myself safe when ,
You hold my hand….
I hope the clock to stop when,
You hold me on ur arms….
I miss the time when,
You make me feel the luckiest one is this world ….life gets better with you….
Being with you is my life….

8. Muralidhar Bansal

Muralidhar Bansal resides in Nepal. He is a businessman at present. He was inspired to write as a student seeing the environment around him. He loves writing as a hobby and he wants to be a good and rational businessman.

@writings_from_heart_92

HOPE

HOPE IS TYPE OF TRUST THAT YOU PLACE ON OTHERS FOR THE BETTER LIFE. BUT THESE DAYS, HOPE SEEMS A DAGGER TO YOURSELF IF OVERDONE.

IT IS SAID HOPE IS GOOD. BUT NOT THE FALSE HOPE. THE HOPE BECOMES FALSE WHEN YOUR EXPECTATIONS FROM OTHERS IS NULL AND VOID.

EVEN THERE IS HOPE IN LOVE. A TRUE HOPE GETS THE EDGES IN LOVE OR ELSE DESPITE SPENDING AGES, YOU CAN'T HAVE A HOPE ON SOMEONE.

HOPE MIGHT BE A GOOD THING. BUT A S IT IS SAID, THE EXCESS OF ANYTHING RUINS YOU. THE EXCESS HOPE LEADS TO DEPENDENCY AND DEPENDENCY SPOILS YOUR CREATIVITY.

HOPE MAY HAVE SOME LIFE. BUT IT HAS NO WINGS. IT MAKE TAKE OFF TO SOME EXTENT. BUT IT CAN'T FLY TO MUCH ALTITUDE.

HOPE IS SAID TO BE A BOON. PEOPLE GET A NEW CHARISMA IN LIFE WITH THE RAYS OF HOPE EVERY MORNING, TO GET A BETTER DAY.

• 19 •

9. Harshita Verma

Co-author Harshita Verma is a writer from Lucknow. She has completed her graduation in commerce stream. She has been writing poetry for the last few years as her passion. She wants to be a novelist in future.

@0___hsh

POSITIVE

Leave the dark days behind

Hope the coming days will bring light

Walk ahead without any fear

Because everything will eventually become clear

Do not suffer because of past

Because that has been long gone

Welcome the new days of life

With utmost gleam and happiness

Pursue your goals with hope

Because they are the one's that will make you happy forever

Be positive as that's the only rule to be happy in the world full of sufferings.

10. Tahreem Afzal

Tahreem Afzal has done her MS in Mathematics. She is the author of "My Soul's Cravings" published by Daastan Publication. She has also worked as Co-author in many anthologies, and currently compiling her own one too. Besides being a dream hunter, she is the girl who is travelling on the path called 'life'. She doesn't complain about the obstacles, she just makes sure that her faith never gets blurry, as this is the only candle of light that keeps her going on dark nights. @Reemsays789

SWEET LIES

You were telling me
How much you love me
You were telling me
That how you adore me
Your words… sugar coated
And your promises…so glittery
I would have really fallen for them
I would have tasted the sweetness
But, all of it seemed to be a lie
When I looked into your eyes
Trying to find myself
Echoing inside you
Your eyes…
They were empty

Like an abandoned forest

That can't offer any luck

I am sorry dear

I couldn't fall for you

I am sorry dear

I can't drown in your barren land

~Believe those eyes that scream of what is really inside, before falling for some lies.

11. Har Deepansh Bahadur Sinha

Har Deepansh Bahadur Sinha belongs to Lucknow, UP. He is a research scholar of Oceanography and has done masters in Geography from National Post Graduate College. He has completed his schooling at Study Hall. His hobbies are art, listening to music, cooking & loads of driving. His interest areas are Astronomy, Writing, Photography & Travelling a lot.

@Deepansh_sinha

BECOMING PARENTS

A newly born child brings immense of happiness
They are the complete package of laziness,
The amount of blood a mother drains
After watching her child she overcomes her pain.
Apart from showing the affection
Fathers are the pillars of protection,
Those visuals are very happening
When your kid starts crawling.
Those who are blessed with twins
Must have committed loads of sins,
So parents wish you infinite laughter
All the best for brand new chapter.

12. RAMYAA K

Ms K. Ramyaa completed her 12th grade and getting ready for her entry into the Medical field by preparing for NEET entrance now. She's a girl who is never afraid to try new things, and she always tries to keep her busy by trying new things like handicrafts, drawings, writings and so on. She already published her debut book as a Co-author. In the world of expecting motivation from the outside, she is the one who tries to made herself as motivation for others. Being positive at any stage of life is her motto. Her favourite quote is "Treat everything equal though it is good or bad".

@creator_29_

THE INVISIBLE CROWN

The invisible crown are the feelings which can be felt but not be seen.

"Optimism is power,

Bliss is shower".

"Both the hands are important to lead a

Life; likewise,

Both POSITIVITY and confidence are two

Helping hands to take us forward

Every time".

"Bliss moments are rare;

But, last long forever..

BLISS is Bless".

"Unknowingly heart cares;

Unlimited affection;
The only thing where we get everything
More than we need—LOVE".
"The realising point;
Time to evaluate;
Time to celebrate us;
Self love will be found in the place where
There is PEACE".(joy)
"The mental strength which is raw material
For the Physical strength—INNER
STRENGTH"

13. Sree Varshini

Sree Varshini was born on 9th August 1996 in Kodaikanal. She loves to write poems and short stories since her school days. She has participated in the International Paper Presentation and won the Best Paper Award. Her poems and short stories were published under around 40 anthologies.

SALTY SMILE

Hot sun, girl on a busy signal,
Selling hanging toys for cars
She ran here and there stood near the window pan
Yellow light, she disappointed
Sat on the roadside corner,
Waiting again for the Red signal
It was on….
Ran towards a vehicle,
A man opened the window,
Bought a doll for his car,
Gave her a hundred rupee note,
Yellow signal
She smiled…..
Sweet smile salty sweat….

14. Noor Tabassum

The name of the author is Noor Tabassum. Writing is her passion. She is an author in Scribe Mag magazine and a blogger in Times of India. She is also a regular poet in Muse India- my space. She has participated in more than 250 anthologies. She has also written solo books called 'Sensibles' and 'Twisted Firsts'. She is a nature lover and loves to lead a simple life. She expresses all her feelings in her writing as she thinks it is the most powerful medium to communicate. Her thoughts and writings are appreciated a lot and she has won many competitions even.

@noortabassumali123

PEACE

I have seen half of the world with pleasure,

Have earned a lot of wealth and treasured,

Have built an enormous palace to live in leisure,

I thought that all these things would give me peace without any pressure.

But I was wrong, my dear,

Peace of mind is the mind-set of a person who lives without fear,

Fear of losing wealth, losing people, losing worldly pleasures mere,

The one who fears to rain the eyes with tears.

All the worldly gains never will give us the desired peace,

For that, we need to keep our heart clean, and then sorrows will seize,

A heart free of jealousy, anger, hatred, dominance, and tease,

Only then will nights bring sound sleep, and tensions will cease.

15. Mohammed Sohail

Mohammed Sohail dwells in Hyderabad, pursuing her B.Sc. He also took part in many anthologies. He loves to explore himself through his pen.
@Sohail_quotes_22

HOPE
Never loose your hope
That you can't achieve any thing
Always be confident
More forward
Peace
Always keep your self in peace
Your angriness may
Destroy your strength

Inner strength
Believe in your self not in others
No one will help in hard times
Your inner strength will help you
Always be confidence
You will be succeeded

16. Maria Johnson

Maria Johnson, also called as Maya. She was born and brought up in Kerala. She has completed her Post Graduation in Accounting and Finance, and currently pursuing Acca & PGDM mainly specializing in Human Resource Management. Maya started her writing career through an online platform named Pratilipi. Her first write-up was a love story – Sainayude Pranayam.

@mariajohnnson

HAPPINESS

Frozen eyes, Depressed mind

Shut down heart ,Fed up tears

Crisp and clear Waiting for my weekend, Rising Anticipation

Hardly waiting for my days of joy & happiness

Let me enjoy this hilarious moment

Watching the fading rain

Have a coffee , take a break,

Settle a smile on my lips

This is what it should be & ought to be

My days of uplifted happiness…

17. Rajashree Bhuyan

Dynamic, bright and charismatic, Rajashree Bhuyan born in the year 2002 in Jorhat, Assam has been awarded the Aspirant Achievers Dr A.P.J Abdul Kalam Award in 2021. She has completed her schooling at Royal Oak High School, Jorhat, Assam and her higher education from Pragya Academy, Jorhat. She is a student of Bachelor of Science, now in Chemistry. Moreover, she is a journalist, speaker, author, compiler of three anthologies, project head and co-author in many anthologies. @Rajashree2700

A REASONING CONCEPT

Peace is a concept of societal friendship and harmony in the absence of hostility and violence. In a social sense, peace is commonly used to mean a lack of conflict (such as war) and freedom from fear of violence between individuals or groups. Peace remains a goal for introspective individuals around the world. The lifelong search for inner peace challenges us to learn more about ourselves while allowing us to evolve with the seasons — and the quotes on our list capture all forms of peace. They'll inspire you to embark on your own journey! After all, creators of past and present would agree that peace requires a journey beginning with you.

18. Mrunmayi Dhage

Mrunmayi Dhageis a graphologist, Vedic maths teacher and a numerologist, Handwriting Teacher, poet writer, drawing the analysis Author handwriting specialist signature specialist social worker.

VIRTUES

Wear your virtues as a crown,

As you walk through life gently,

And with grace, think for yourself…aloud

You possess a beauty much more than queenly

In your eyes … is heaven

In your heart…love and compassion

Dance in your steps

And magic on your fingertips…

Go placidly through noise and chaos

Remember you are 'the gift'…

Just be okay with "YOU"

And make of your life a gift

19. SHEHARAJ KHAN

Sheharaj hails from Mumbai Thane, and she's pursuing her B.Sc. degree. Apart from writing poetry, Sheharaj is a handwriting specialist, teacher of maths and drawing, and a social worker.
@_xstancekhan1x_

FREE HAPPINESS
The best thing about happiness,
It is free…
If anyone can't make you happy
Than how someone make you sad
The way to make yourself happy
To love yourself…
Don't lose hope
If you have hard problem in life
Show that you are more harder than it..

20. Rimjhim Agrawal

Rimjhim Agrawal was born on 16th April 2003. She lives in GKP, Utter Pradesh. She loves helping others, chiefly because when she needed a support, she found none and hence she knows the pain. Her writings are just the way of expressing her feelings. She has written 30+ anthologies and she loves to sing ,dance, cook, and to have a good sense of humour.

@Rimjhimagrawal409

DON'T LET

Don't let anyone hurts you physical or mentally it's all depends on you

Don't let anyone make you feel unlike from others it's their thinking not yours

Don't let anyone disrespect you over and over again Bcoz self respect is important

Don't let anyone take ur life decision Bcoz it's your life not their life

Don't let anyone can ever destroy ur peace of mind when you are happy with ur

Love ones ♥?

21. Dr. Roopa Pareek

Dr. Roopa Pareek is the wife of Dr. Uma Shankar. Her Educational Qualifications are as follows: M.Sc.(in Physics), M.Ed. Ph. D.(Edu.). She has experience of 36 years in different fields like teaching Physics ,Educational Research, being the Head of the Educational Institution (School), and the Master facilitator for Leadership Training of Head of the School etc. She has been awarded as the Best Teacher. To her, story writing, acting, anchoring gives so much pleasure to her. Her son serves in an INDIAN Army(??). Her published books are "Khil uthi hai Prarthana" Poetry, " pankh jinse koi uda the" story Book. Language Hindi.

EMANCIPATION

Everyone knows the fact who is wise

If there is entrance there is exit likewise.

Everybody seeking liberty and happiness.

Everybody leave this world later or sooner

Everybody wants to be loved by someone.

But very few know how to deserve

People dislike the hindrance but few know

By enjoying the restriction one can achieve

EMANCIPATION

22. Gayathri Tamilselvan

Gayathri Tamilselvan who goes by her pen name Selna M Gayath, is a writer of no particular genre. She writes poems, short stories, novels and what not. Her debut poetry collection, 'PENniyal' is out for purchase. Her novels are available on Wattpad. She likes little things. She is a simple girl – a simple girl with huge dreams.
@gayathri_tamilan

JUST YOU
When I first laid
My eyes on you,
It didn't rain or storm
Or shake or scorch.
The world went on
By its business.
It showed no signs
Of any nonsense.
I didn't have a hint
I'd ever love you.
I didn't fall or rise in love.
I just loved you with all my love.
No, I'm not a realist.
I do comparisons.
I've compared you
With that last drop

Of my already cold coffee –

Cold yet I taste it.

I've compared you

To a bourbon biscuit –

Less brownie

But sweeter than the biscuit.

See, I do comparison of my own.

After all, I own you –

One in a million

And it is only appropriate

To use comparisons

That are at least one in a thousand.

23. Mohammed Niyaz

Mohammed Niyaz hails from Mumbai – The City Of Dreams. He often loves to write poetry and short music, video, and stories for his YouTube channel. Apart from these, Mohammed is currently working on his upcoming anthologies, as well as writing poetry since 2013. @niyazsks

(Quote 1)

Life is a bunch of stages under motions.

We need to calm down and secure the rest of it.

Our feelings as well the denominations we hold.

This is what we need to uplift for the betterment of our own purpose.

(Quote 2)

Stay strong, stay dedicated towards your target.

Mistakes and flaws doesn't matter where you are.

But the time you count yourselves in the most wanted scenarios.

I swear you will conclude the kingdom of struggles.

(Quote 3)

Human beings has emotions of loads apart.

They being insane from the opposites of attractions.

Tears and fears combines them in a sight of strength.

Securing the best of surrounds they deserves.

24. Hritik Prasad

Hritik Prasad lives in Samastipur. He's an introvert but a little bit. He believes that karma decides the faith of every person, so we have to do our best in any field. He wrote in many anthologies regularly but sometimes got his thoughts and try to put it in notes. In his view, being alone make the readers feeling happy and he loves to spend time alone . One of his best motivational is in Mrinal bhaiyaa, in which he faced a lots of problems but never left hope.

@Hritik_pd

LIFE IS LIKE

Life is running like a wind.
People became cunning as they are rich,
It's being difficult to find some peace.
Anger in everyone minds,
It's difficult to be a reason behind any smile,
Life became lie, happiness seems to be flied.
And then mind decides, to feel a vibe around
Make my heart listen that peaceful sound.
That will make you remind,
You are not the one who struggle for their own.
Life is running like a wind,
It's difficult to find some peace,
It's seems to be out of reach.
Life is running like a wind.

25. Neha

Neha hails from Samastipur, Bihar. She is the daughter of Usha Kumari, whom she loves so much. She is totally in love with Lord Krishna, truly believes that nothing is impossible in this world if you have faith in lord Krishna. To her, He is the mentor, director of life and everything. Neha loves to travel and enjoy the world.
@Its_ahana_n

U WILL MISS ME
One day, you missed me ? And called me
And asked me ?
Did u missed me I missed you today.
I replied with a pleasant smile .
No I didn't missed you
I Just remembered you .
When the sun rises till the sunset, I missed you when I breathe, I missed you when I walk , talk.
Sun fade away stars came on my way .
I called you were busy you asked me to put the phone as you are feeling dizzy ,
I leaved my hope, and tried hard to elope.
And I stopped thinking some peaceful sound and that will someday remind and
One day you will miss me .

26. SNEHA PRIYA

Sneha hails from Singhia Khurd, Samastipur, Bihar. Her other name is Muskan. She is the daughter of Vijendra Kumar and Manisha Kumar and the loving sister of Snehil. She loves to write whenever she's joyful. Apart from writing, she loves shopping and her chief goal in life is to make everyone happy and peaceful.

@Mussu.1018

DEAR LOVE

Love you till my last breathe,

You loved me without any need,

You cared for me crossing all boundaries,

Made me feel sunshine in life ,

I wanna see the world with your sight ,

Now I realise my mom was always right,

Thinking about you make me delight,

I wanna spend my life under that beautiful moon light.

Dear love you are my strength,

Br with me till my last breathe,

Hold me tight, staying with you make me feel everything is right.

27. Riya Richard R. L

Riya Richard R. L is a young, burgeoning writer in English. She has adored writing since her girlhood. She has a unique style and distinct modus operandi in her writings- poems, quotes, short stories, novels, etc… She has worked as a Co-author in 500+ anthologies. She is involved in Compiling and has Compiled three anthologies. Her first anthology published is 'Courage to Continue'. She is from Kanyakumari district, Tamil Nadu. She is now an undergraduate in Chemistry. Besides writing, she also loves reading books, drawing, arts and crafts, and learning. She is a lover of Nature.
@rl.riya21

THE ONE REASON
The World gave me
Hundreds of reasons to Cry,
The World gave me
Thousand reasons to Worry,
The World gave me,
Ten thousand reasons to Weep,
The World gave me,
Lakhs of reasons to Sob,
The World gave me,
Millions of reasons to Mourn,
But I had one Reason to Smile,
Being Optimistic over Distress!

28. Muskan Kesarwani

Muskan Kesarwani is a resident of Pragraj Katghar. She likes to write and she always writes from her heart and she has expressed her heartfelt gratitude to her dear friends. She used to love writing and have kept it as a hobby, with the great support of her family and siblings. According to her, every person has some dreams fulfilled, and yet she worked hard in the process of writing and so far, she has participated in more than 200 anthologies and now she desires to publish her book. @heartless_mussu

INNER STRENGTH

Faith can move mountains and heal wounded hearts;

Beauty will linger where're hope imparts; Love can bring comfort when life seems too tough; But, when day is finished, strength shall be enough. Inner strength is a fortress where sanity reigns,

A pillar of peace, far from grief and pain, A place where the sunlight so effortlessly shines,

Enshrouding the spirit in warmth, undefined. In each moral fabric, one thing remains clear,

Through times of much hardship,

Strength falls with each tear; Thus, with every teardrop, the soul shall be cleansed, Thanks to inner strength and support from true friends.

No moment of struggle, marred by loss or grief,

Shall ever be greater than the wide belief, That every challenge has reason to come,

For each heart is tailored to never succumb. Inner strength is our light through a forest of trees, Guiding our way, always, with the greatest of ease, Embracing our purpose, down each earthen trail.

• 45 •

29. Yukta Sri CK

Yukta Sri CK is an 18 years old engineering student, pranic healer, poetess and writer. She has co-authored several books and the light is her language! You can reach her on Instagram @high_on_clairvoyance_
@high_on_clairvoyance_

PLAN B

Do we all need a plan B ?

Absolutely , yes

You may say that isn't a winners attitude

But to me your only plan A must be is to make it to the summit

You may choose different paths to get there,

but the thing is to be on the high

May be the path one which you selected to travel has a sink hole ?

Will you sink and vanish forever?

So what if you didn't have a plan B?

Then you will be lost on your way

It's okay if the second path has thorns

They'll make you bleed,

Of course you will have to bleed to reach the summit

But isn't this path of thorn

the safest than path with the sink hole?

If you didn't have a plan B

of choosing the path of thorns

Then you would have either disappeared in the sink hole or stuck before it

Your plan B is your life line!

Don't ask what if plan B fails!

Look for the other path

You know it now

You will to make it to the summit!

30. Adila Firoz

Adila Firoz is a final year student pursuing Bachelor's degree in English. She hails from "The God's Own Country" Kerala. She has won numerous accolades in academic, cultural and literary events. She has worked with a couple of anthologies and has explored the literary arena by getting her poems, essays, short stories and articles published. She has also presented research papers in National and International Conferences. Besides, she is a debater, orator, communication trainer, critical thinker and an artist.

@_adila_firoz_

THE UNSUNG HERO

There's this man
Who has a fire in mind and at heart
The Unsung Hero
With a kind heart
"Let me be by your side",
"Let me help you"—
He wouldn't even budge
To accept these fruits
I love him from the heart
I wanna win his trust
And earn his love
I respect the genuine soul
Let me have his heart

But not to break it into two
He is gonna be great one day
He is great already
The Unsung Hero
With the invisible crown and scythe
Who won my heart
Which wishes not to part ways ever.

31. Abhishek Singh Parcha

Abhishek Singh Parcha is a stenographer who loves to write and read poems as well. He lives in Kamal Park, Delhi, he does rapper lyrics and poetry. His inspiration to write these content have come from Dr. Rahat Indori Sahab.

@Abhishek_singh_parcha

A CONVERSATION
Today my lucky two,
Give doubt to my lover.
Of conversation with conversation,
What to do to have a relationship with Rakib.
It's on the list
Is in the table.
And I am one
Tola the last morsel
When you walk with me, God Kosi
You are the fate of common fire.
He is looking,
I see in God.
And to come,
In your eyes and
A liar is a liar.
Laughing and said that my love is married, will not be happy.

32. Rozy Paul

Rozy Paul belongs to the tea estate called Dibrugarh, Assam. She has completed her M.A.in Journalism. Her hobbies are reading, gardening and cooking. She likes writing a lot. Her favourite saying is 'live and let live'.

@rozypaul

WILL POWER

"Inner strength is much stronger than outer strength if your will power is so strong and you put your cent percent to the work then nobody can stop you to reach the goal."

Optimistic-"Optimism is the way of life. Because all doors are not closed and there is cause behind every failure who understand this they wake up again and search his/her own way to get success in life. Being sad in failure or struggle time is just wasting time rather work on own self to be established."

Self-confidence-"Confidence is the key to uplift own self and portray to the best of all among others. To show the world your own calibre you need to make sure own self that yes I have that much material which can convince others to be best amongst all."

33. K.Eswari

Miss K.Eswari hails from Virudhunagar. She has completed her Bachelor's Degree in English Literature at V.V.Vannia Perumal College, Virudhunagar and currently doing her Bachelor of Education (B.Ed) in Srividya College of Education under (TNTEU). She's an awesome motivational speaker and a great optimist. She has co-authored nearly 80 anthologies (both Tamil and English). She's one of the awardees in the Blue Star Awards. Her way of describing words are very much optimistic. In addition, she is interested in drawing, is a nice singer and an awesome cook. She is the best inspiration to many and a good supporter. She dreams to become a great realistic writer in future as a simple girl with lots of dreams.
@eswarikumaran2311

OPTIMISM

You are…

My great friend!

You gift me awesome vibes!

You gift me lot of victories!

You are the treasure house of enthusiasm!

You are the treasure box of happiness!

You are the best motivator!

My best warrior!

The great pillar of my dreams!

Gift me awesome self confidence!

Gift me lots and lots of victories!
I'm nothing without you!

34. Charishma Jaikishin Ramchandani

Charishma Jaikishin Ramchandani is a poet and writer hailing from Pune, Maharashtra – India. She has completed her Masters in English Literature in 2016, Montessori Teacher's Training in 2017 and her B.Ed degree in 2020. She has worked in India and in the Middle East in Oman as well. Haiku poetry is very dear to her. She has been published in leading haiku magazines, e-zines, newspapers, various anthologies, etc. She has practiced Pythagorean Numerology, Vastu, Panic healing, Runes, Tarot Card reading, Reiki, Pendulum Dowsing, Crystal therapy, Feng Shui and many more metaphysical sciences. She is currently pursuing her Masters in Philosophy from IGNOU besides being very occupied by her 16 months old son, Soham, who, along with Mother Nature, is the inspiration behind her poetry. @Charishma520808

INFINITE STRENGTH

Durga Devi, Oh All-mighty Goddess,
With infinite strength, Oh rider of lions.
From dawn to dusk with prayers sincere,
I beseech You to grant me my baby dear.
With Your name on my moist lips,
Doing good deeds I seek Your blessings.
No soul I wish to harm, Oh Mother.

35. Pragati Sharma

Pragati Sharma is a teenager from New Delhi. She is currently pursuing her high school degree from Sadhu Vaswani International School for Girls. According to Pragati, it was Ms Seerat, who always encouraged her to explore and discover herself more by participating in various competitions. Her other teacher, Ms Jaspreet Kaur also helped her out with her writing styles. She helped her on how to grab the attention of the audience and how to make her write-ups even more intriguing.

Many of her write-ups are about the inequalities faced by women domestically, verbally, inside their houses and outside.

STRAIGHT FROM MY HEART TO YOURS

At this time of melancholy

Where the breeze of gloom

And corona has locked us in our homes

And our lives like that of caged birds

The roads are totally vacant

Schools and colleges are locked

Restraunts and theatres , malls

All are closed due to this pandemic

We are being sulky day by day

We are yearning for being free

The number of patients

And deaths are amplifying

We are being insane
Our bliss has been hindered
We are in an era of arduous ambiguity
We need to be mindful and meticulous
As the danger is menacing all the time
But soon we shall be free
The roads would be again chock blocked
People will travel again
across the countryside and overseas
And again shall the classrooms cheer up.

36. Hema Kirthiga J.

J. Hema Kirthiga's pen name is Hyson. She is professionally a psychologist and passionately a writer. She heals others but writing heals her. She is a writer, reader, orator and a believer. She is from Chennai. She lives by the principle of inspiring and being inspired. She writes her heart and soul and she deeply believes that the depth of her heart and the nib of her pen are soulfully connected. Writing is an art and she is a proud artist. She loves what she does and loves what she writes.

@The_pen_queen

LIFE!!!

Fight not until you loss!

But until you win!

Work hard to achieve,

Work smart to progress!

Choose a goal,

Plan your path,

Know yourself,

Walk on the way!

Until you achieve.

Let the world know who you are!

Never fight them with words!

But slap them with success!

Life is not the sweetest, Know the bitterness so that you can enjoy the sweetness!

Fight for it! Achieve what you start! Leaving in the middle is the worst thing you can do!

Hope! Plan! Fight! Win!

37. Blessan Blandena

Blessan Blandena is a 17 years old aspiring writer. She is currently pursuing her B.Tech. She mainly writes about her life and her gender. She had her writings submitted in almost 90+ anthologies. @blessan_blandena

YOU AND YOU

I still remember the dress you wore when we first met

That stunning blue satin Ghaghara

It made me fall for you

Those Innocent eyes that kept searching for me

That walk that made everyone stare at you

The sun was never that brighter before

Everyone's eyes were on You

But Your eyes were searching for my stupid soul

Your voice shivered when you said a hi to me

I still remember that big bright smile you had after catching my gaze

I still remember how my heart beat raised

But trust me I feel the same every time.

38. MS. ANANYA BHATTACHARYYA

Cool and mesmerizing Ananya Bhattacharyya was born and brought up in Assam. She is now a Post Graduate student of Dibrugarh University, Assam. She is a passionate singer and also has an aptitude for writing. She loves art too. She is a sandwich lover. She believes in thinking globally act locally.

@arisinganne

INNER STRENGTH

No, I can't do this!

This is just impossible for me.

No, I must try for once!

But if I will fail then how can I recover?

No, failure is the pillar of success.

I can do this!

I must try, I must try!

Oh! It's so hard,

How can I approach?

I must go back, I can't do this.

I want to leave this task.

No, I must approach!

I can do this!

I will succeed, I will surely succeed!

Yes, I accomplished it!

I am a winner!
My decision was right,
I must not quit in life.
I am a winner!
I am stronger than I think;
I am stronger, I am winner!

39. Yasir Ali Durrani

His name is Yasir Ali Durrani.He is Currently Doing his Doctor Of Pharmacy. He has worked as Co-author in many Anthologies and does writing especially Poetry as a passion without the greed of any money. He writes because he loves to write and whenever he feels to write. He loves to embrace and overcome challenges of life and that's what makes him special because it widens up his view of seeing the world and keeps him for to think of.
@_misfitwanderz

SWEET OR BITTER?!
Sweet in her own way
Bitter in her own
Sweet to show love
Sweet when beneath
The full moon listening
To my heart murmurs
Bitter to show love
Bitter to protect me
Bitter to prevent the scars
That tear my heart out
Sweet or Bitter?!
Maybe both yet still
Mine and for me

40. SANSKRITI YADAV

Sanskriti is a writer by habits and an actress by heart. She considers helping needy people her duty. She considers art as her sole Karma. @sanskriti__rao

TO ALL THE DOGS I'VE LOVED

To all the dogs I've loved before,

You were not like my pet,

I had the strongest connection with you

You all were my soulmate.

To all the pups who played on my lap,

You were like my own child,

My heart bloomed out of happiness

Whenever you smiled.

The days when I screamed silently;

My dogs didn't eat,

The nights I wept to bed;

My dogs didn't sleep.

I am sorry to all the stray dogs

I couldn't provide a shelter,

You treated me as your master

But I was a mere helper.

I am sorry to all the stranger dogs

I poked without a reason,

Yes you felt to me like my own

I never understood the division.
Your tongues were the best wipes to my tears.
Your fur was the best blanket to my fears.
Your hugs were the best medicine to my wound
I wish to have a similar shroud,
Your paws are imprinted on my heart
Our relationships were deep but too short!
I wanna spend my life with your hand in mine
I know this sounds absurd and new
But no human can love me the way you do
And I wish I could marry you!

41. K.A JANNATHUL FIRDOUS

Jannathul Firdous is pursuing her Bachelor of Arts Degree in English Literature and is more passionate about books and writings. She's skilful in exposing her sparkles through her words by making the world as optimistic lands.

MICRO TALE

Young girl eager for opportunity, she is delightful with her talent in writing and typing. Life went like jazz music more rhythmic, during a day felt a shine in the sky outside the window in night the Dazzle moon sparkled her dreams, unfortunately the gloom state covered her Shine Sky because of a mother who was in Ill state due to nerve problem that deeply affected at peace, counting days it last for months drowning hope and happiness, pain of losing opportunity close the windows. This time Window Viewed the dark rain. One day cloud will pass, Rainbow will raise.

42. MUBEEN TAJ. M

Mubeen Taj is pursuing her final year in the Bachelor's Degree of Arts in English literature. She loves to write many poems and short stories. She loves reading and she enjoys writing poems.

THE SILENT LANGUAGE

A hundred years old weaving loom
Speaking the most silent language of all
Turning threads into lyrical lines
And turning cotton blend,
Into poetic polyester verses
About hourglass days passing by
And love declarations turning into
A lost passing ship
Waving with a goodbye sail
Time ticking away
With a storytelling rhythm
Winding of wool words
And every satin syllabus stitch
Containing the hope for a final design
That embodies soothing cashmere
Telling a happy ending after all.

43. Muskan Taj

The Co-author Muskan Taj is studying in 12th (intermediate) in commerce stream, hailing from Bangalore, in the country India. Her aim is to become a business woman. As the sky have no limit, her goal is to achieve many things in her life. Her realistic vision is to dream, and make it a goal and she never stops aiming high, and she never stops till she gets there. She finds every little opportunity to learn something new. Her success is in small victories, and she works hard for it.

@kuls745

LOVE

When I suddenly realized,

How much I need you in my life

When I think I will never see you again.

I miss you again and again

There is something miraculous about you.

I don't know what's in your presence

That

Makes me so happy.

When you hold me firmly in your arms.

And whisper in my ear:

"I love you and miss you too"

And I don't want to let you go.

So that you become part of me.

And I became part of you.

44. Rushabh kharade

Rushabh kharade hails from the city of diamonds, and he is just trying to bring peace to souls of human beings around him.
@Kharade_sahab

I HATE MY ALARM

I remember, I was dreaming…maybe!

But I saw her in my world! Before starting let me tell you my world doesn't have anything special just a beach with sparkling sand in night and a cool breeze with a pleasant smell, A sky full with twinkling starts and a full moon

She was like one's who can mesmerize anyone, I the second movement I just pinched my self to see I was dreaming or not and the answer was yes I was dreaming and many other things were there in my mind but she

She was chewing a gum, in bit of a boyish charm, she looked at someone and smiled with the innocence of a little girl

She was asking someone what is this place

In a shuttle yet clear voice

I remember she was having a Smokey greyish eyes and a nose ring. Her cheeks were as pink as cherry blossom and her hairs where tangled that its every strang waves at different directions.

She came to me and was trying to asking me something but being nervous I mumbled something only I can understand And she just smiled at me as if this was a daily occurrence for her but for me it was completely new. She was so different from what you see regularly in the crowd.

I remember she was having a sexy tattoo on her neck and also her face that can bend any guy to knees , if someone try to drop hints by the time she could actually come and talk about it directly.

She doesn't think before doing anything and when she talks, she looks fairly into your eyes that can make you forget what you where talking about and when the movement comes When I was actually going to say something to her, gathering my all courage and try to make conversations in my mind about the ways in which I will talk to her which also includes a try to impress her but then in between all this things suddenly I heard a sound which was buzzing and interrupting between my conversation try, shaking and shattering everything which I was seeing and in another second I saw her fading after that everything just disappeared in a blink and I woke up with broken dream looking to my alarm and cursing it with all my heart.

45. Vaishnawi Kumari

Vaishnawi Kumari is the co-author of 10+ world record anthologies along with 200+ successful creations with different publications. Her books have received praise and recognition from many well-known publications. This gorgeous poetess belongs to Patna, Bihar, and she is an upcoming computer science graduate from NSIT, Bihta, Patna. After being motivated by his father, she has sharpened her passion for writings as well as dancing and singing. There are 6+ upcoming projects as an author. She believes that poetry can change the world, and she uses it to inspire and empower young people through it. You can personally contact with her Instagram handle @kumarivaishnawi and can follow @mystic.vaishu to see her amazing creations. @Mystic.vaishu

MY HAPPINESS: FATHER

Everyone gives importance to the mother,

But why does one forget the father and his struggle,

Who is the roof of our house,

Why does he leave them apart,

Why do we forget what the father did for us,

He earn some little money by filling our stomach,

He fulfilled our every need by ignoring his need….

Why we do not know the story of a father.?

Why the eyes are not able to see the struggle of the father.?

Do you need a mother to live life, not a father?

If the mother is heaven, then the father has lost the observance of that heaven…
I am thankful to the god who gave me such a father…
Who loves me more than everyone else,
What is the story of a father to me is not unknown,
I am fine with their struggle and understand their situation,
Open your eyes a little, understand the struggle of a father, if a mother is necessary in life, then a father is equally important.

46. Shubhanjali Nishad

Shubhanjali Nishad hails from Kanpur. Writing is her strength, and she writes in every mood. Her hobbies are reading books, writing, travelling. She has passed out her graduation from CSJM University. She cares much and works hard now on upcoming anthologies. She has also co-authored 50+ anthologies. Her chief aim in life is to achieve success. In a short time, she has penned Shayari, poetry and articles by heart because she knows very well the imagination of writers are better than their dreams. She is a blessing from Lord Krishna and she wholly believes in karma.
@Painfull_lafz13

OPTIMISTIC

No matter what outside, I am strong inside

I recognize my merit by my ability

Because I have passion and Faith in my work.

So now I complete my work easily.

I am optimistic I never give up hope

I know how to ease all my difficulties

I know my inner strength very well

The lamp of hope should

Always be kept lit in the mind.

What am I know this very well I

Like a lamp has faith in its wick

Like a Sun shine I Will shine do this

Same way I believe in my mind

That I can do every difficult task easily

I keep a confidence in my mind

I will done all work with the self-confidence of my mind

• 74 •

47. Allish Chaudhary

Allish Chaudhary is a twenty-five year old girl, pursuing Masters, from Dilwalo Ki Apni Delhi, New Delhi, India. She is an emotional writer, slowly and gradually gaining interest in writing. And now she is here immensely happy and proud to introduce her another official write up. There's a quote which says, "Paper has more patience than Human", (she is totally in love with this quote and feeling this quote damn true after writing).
@words.stream

SORRY TO YOU

We were too close, Still together but not so close, Trust was there,
But now just fight is here, How can I prove myself?
That I m not a liar, Trust me once , May be we will be again close to each other ,
Can't live with your resentment, It is a big punishment,
U were trying , But I was also not telling lie ,
I m short tempered , But just because I knew u r always there,
Don't take me wrong , Never think anything about u wrong,
I knew I m wrong , But don't leave my hand , Because I m not so strong ,
Can't understand everything at my own , U r introvert- I m extrovert ,
But m not able to express myself to anyone, U will get so many frnds,
But I have only one (You), Want to say sorry, With love to the only one (You).

The End